W9-CZV-035

GLASSBORO STATE COLLEGE

ERUDITIO SPES MUNDI

1923

NEW JERSEY

SAVITZ LIBRARY

GLASSBORO, NEW JERSEY

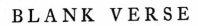

BLANK VERSE

BLANK VERSE

BY

JOHN ADDINGTON SYMONDS

AMS PRESS
NEW YORK

PE
1515
S8
1970

Reprinted from the edition of 1895, New York
First AMS EDITION published 1970
Manufactured in the United States of America

International Standard Book Number: 0-404-06328-4

Library of Congress Card Catalog Number: 74-119657

AMS PRESS, INC.
NEW YORK, N.Y. 10003

3 3001 00573 6342

PREFACE

THIS Volume is published in obedience to the wishes of Mr. J. A. SYMONDS, thus expressed: "There are three Essays upon English Blank Verse, printed in small type as an Appendix to my *Sketches and Studies in Italy*. In that place they have been entirely lost to sight and observation. They ought to be taken out and published separately in a small volume."

HORATIO F. BROWN.

Sept. 1894.

146624

CONTENTS

I

PREFATORY NOTE

Ancient metre depends on quantity, modern metre on accent—
Decay of sense of quantity even in classical times—English
verse depends on accent—Distinction between quantity and
accent—Pause and elision—Lines scanned by accent less
precise than lines scanned by quantity—Hence the licence
of Blank Verse—Quantitative scansion of Blank Verse is not a
right canon of criticism—Complexity of the whole question
of metre—The best craftsmen work by instinct

II

THE HISTORY OF BLANK VERSE

Varied and plastic quality of English Blank Verse—Limitation of
the iambic by the Greeks—Sackville and Norton introduce
Blank Verse—Marlowe's " Tamburlaine "—Blank Verse per-
fected by Marlowe—His exuberance and variety—Shakspere
—Musical quality of his verse—His freedom from mannerism
— Ben Jonson—Beaumont and Fletcher — Marston — Other
Elizabethan Dramatists—Licence of Webster—His justification
—Milton—Decadence of Blank Verse—Dryden—Thomson—
Cowper—Coleridge—Wordsworth—Byron—Revival of Blank
Verse by Keats — and Shelley — Browning — Swinburne —
Tennyson — Tennyson's mastery of the metre — General
considerations of the scope of Blank Verse—Blank Verse
only the metre of genius .

CONTENTS

III

THE BLANK VERSE OF MILTON

BLANK VERSE

I

PREFATORY NOTE

A SENTENCE in an essay on England's literary debt to Italy furnishes me with a pretext for reprinting two separate studies on Blank Verse.* They were composed with a view to illustrating the rhetoric rather than the prosody of this metre, on the conviction that, though Blank Verse is an iambic rhythm, it owes its beauty to the liberties taken with the normal structure. The licences allowed

---

* I have not attempted to avoid repetitions in these Essays. The three parts were written at intervals during the last ten years; and two of them have been separately published. My purpose will be sufficiently served by a simple reprint, and I trust that the reader will not be fatigued by occasional recapitulation of the points I have sought to establish.

themselves in this metre by great masters of versification may be explained, I think, invariably when we note the accent required by the rhetorical significance of their abnormal lines.

It can fairly be argued, however, that with this end in view I have paid too little attention to the prosody of Blank Verse, or, in other words, to its scansion by feet. In order to meet this objection, some prefatory remarks may here be offered upon the difficult question of quantity and accent.

We are accustomed, roughly speaking, to say that ancient metre depends on Quantity and modern metre on Accent. The names Dactyl, Spondee, Trochee, &c., were invented in the analysis of Greek metres to express certain combinations of long and short syllables, without reference to pitch or emphasis. But when we speak of Quantity in English metre, we mean the more or less accentuation of syllables. Thus an English trochee is a foot in which the first syllable is more accen-

tuated than the second ; an iamb is the contrary. In the transition from the ancient to
the modern world the sense of Quantity seems
to have been lost, and its values were replaced
by Accent. We find, for example, in the
watch-song of the Modenese soldiers, which
can be referred to a period about the middle
of the tenth century, such iambics as the
following :

> Divina mundi rex Christe custodia,
> Sub tua serva haec castra vigilia.

Both lines have an accentual as well as a
quantitative trochee in the fourth place. In
the second line the accents on the first
syllable of *tua*, and on the second syllable of
vigilia, which would have been too slight to
lengthen them for a classical bar, are allowed
to supply the place of quantity.

If Latin verses could thus be written without attention to quantity, this shows that the
feeling for it had expired; and even at a
period which may still be called classical, the
gradual blunting of the sensibility can be

traced in the shortening of vowel sounds. It will suffice to quote the following hexameter :

Caetera mando focis spernunt quae dentes acuti.

The Pompeian *graffiti* prove abundantly that among the common people at any rate it had never been acute ; and we are led to the conclusion that scansion by quantity in Latin was an artificial refinement, agreeable to highly educated ears. When, therefore, we proceed to state that English lines ignore quantity, we mean that the cultivated feeling for the relative values of long and short syllables has never been sufficiently vivid with us to make us particular about preserving them. We are satisfied with the values afforded by accentuation, though there is no doubt that verses can be written with correct accentuation which shall also preserve quantity in the classic sense. Tennyson's experiments in Alcaics, Hendecasyllabics, and Sapphics suffice for proof. The difference between us and the cultivated ancients in this respect may, in a measure, be due to our comparatively negligent pronunciation. For instance, we do not pronounce the word *mella* as the Italians do, so as to give the full value to both *l*'s. We have not trained our ear to require, or our vocal organs to make, that delicate differentiation of syllables according to their spelling—in other words, to separate instead of slurring the component parts of speech—on which quantity depends. These considerations lead to a theory of metrical analysis which may be offered with some diffidence.

The laws of metre are to be found in the natural rhythm of words; for each word in every language has its own rhythmical form. This natural rhythm is expressed in pronunciation, and is determined by the greater or less time consumed in the enunciation of the syllables. Quantity and Accent distinguish two conditions of this expenditure. Quantity, apart from Accent, is the measure of time lengthened or abbreviated, necessary for the due articulation of the component parts of language. Thus, generally speaking, a long syllable is one in which double vowels or a vowel before accumulated consonants demand a full time for their utterance; a short syllable is one in which a single vowel or a vowel before a simple consonant may be uttered in a half time. *Me* (double *e*) and *Tunc* are long: *Que* (single *e*) and *Sub* are short. It is agreed, apparently, in European metres to take account only of full and half times; yet much of the more subtle rhythmical effects depends upon the relative values of syllables which can only be conventionally regarded as not exceeding or falling short of one of the two limitations. Not every long is of exactly equal length. Not every short is of exactly equal brevity. Accent is indifferently used to indicate two separate conditions. It is either the measure of intonation, heightened or lowered, or else it is enforced utterance. Of the former sort of accent, or pitch, which probably played an important part in Greek versification, no account need at present be taken. The latter, or *ictus*, has the effect of quantity, inasmuch as it renders more time needful for the stress laid upon the syllable—the accumulated volume of sound requiring a greater effort of the vocal organs, and consequently a retarded utterance. Every word, then, in articulation is subject to conditions of time, implying what we call Quantity and Accent; and in many words quantity is hardly distinguishable from accent. Thus, in the line :

Tityre tu patulae recubans sub tegmine fagi,

the quantity of *Tityre* can be represented either as a double vowel followed by two simple vowels, requiring a time and two half times for enunciation, or else as an antepenultimate accent. Without pursuing this analysis into further details, it may be possible to define Quantity as enunciation retarded or accelerated by the greater or less simplicity of the sound to be formed by the vocal

7

organs; Accent as the retardation of a simple
sound by the increased effort of the vocal
organs needed for marking the *ictus*. They
are both, so to speak, in the category of
time; and though it is necessary to distinguish them, it should not be forgotten that
their importance in prosody is due to the
divisions and subdivisions of time they
represent.

The consideration of Pause and Elision
will help to illustrate these definitions. When
two strong consonants have to be pronounced
together, there must always be a pause
between them, and with the pause an expenditure of time. That is the secret of the
quantity ascribed to the preceding vowel.
Thus *amor* in *amor est* has the value of ‿‿,
because no pause is needed, no second consonantal sound being produced after its
pronunciation; in *amor dans* it has the value
of ‿‒, because a fresh consonant has to be
formed. The English do not mark this
pause clearly. In other words, they do not

give full value to each consonant, especially when the same letter is repeated. The Italians do: the first syllable of *mellifluo*, for instance, must be articulated *mel'-lifluo*; and so jealous is the spirit of the language on this point that in words like *accento* the value of the double *cc* is preserved by a *t'-ch* sound. It may be asserted that in proportion as the pronunciation of syllables in a language is more or less perfect, in the same proportion will the sense for quantity be vivid, and quantitative versification be easy.

Elision can be explained on the same principles. Since no fresh effort, no pause, no new expenditure of time is needed when two vowels come together, they are suffered to pass as one. How true a law this is may be perceived when we remember that vulgar persons introduce an *r* between two *a*'s, owing to the difficulty of otherwise articulating them separately. The Lucretian elision of the final *s* in words like *moenibus*, before a consonant, probably shows that this final sibilant was on the point of becoming mute ; and the recognised elision of *m* in words like *mecum* before a vowel may in like manner indicate that this liquid had become practically mute, *mecum* tending toward the modern *meco.*

The main drift of the foregoing analysis has been to show that both Quantity and Accent have a common element of Time. It consequently follows that metres which, like the English, practically ignore quantity, can be scanned in feet, or divided into bars, by accent. Yet the result will never be so accurate as in the case of quantitative rhythms, chiefly because accent itself is variable with us ; and the same combinations of syllables, by a slight shifting of accents, may appear to one observer a dactyl, to another an anapæst, and so forth.

An instance may be furnished by the following line, which is a passable hendecasyllabic Blank Verse:

She in her hands held forth a cup of water.

If we accentuate the first syllable, the
rhythm would most naturally be marked thus:

$$- \cup \cup \mid -- \mid - \cup \mid - \cup \mid - \bar{\cup} \mid$$

But this does not yield even a "licentiate
iambic." Therefore, in order to bring it within
the rule of the metre, we must shift the accent
and scan :

$$\cup - \mid \cup - \mid -- \mid \cup - \mid \cup - \bar{\cup} \mid$$

It is of no use to complain that the line
is a bad one, and ought to be re-written,
because similar lines are of plentiful occurrence in our best dramatic writers. Without
such irregularities, Blank Verse would be
monotonous.

Licences which would have been intolerable
to a Greek ear, such as successive trochees in
the third and fourth places, of which there are
several specimens in Milton, or a trochee in
the second place, which is a favourite expedient
of Shelley's, are far from disagreeable in the
English iambic. Indeed, so variable is its

structure that it is by no means easy to define the minimum of metrical form below which a Blank Verse ceases to be a recognisable line. It is possible that the diminution of the English iambic by one foot less than the Greek renders its licences more tolerable, and facilitates that interweaving of successive lines by which so many discords are resolved in a controlling harmony. Lastly, it may be observed that, being an accentual metre, blank verse owes much of its rhythmical quality to emphasis. For emphasis is but enforced accent; and when the proper emphasis has been discovered in a line, the problem of its rhythmical structure has almost always been solved. It is thus that close attention to the rhetoric of Blank Verse becomes absolutely necessary.

It will be seen from the foregoing observations that I am neither for nor against the method of scanning Blank Verse by the traditional feet of Greek and Latin metres. The terms of ancient prosody represent per-

manent relations between syllables, nor is
there anything merely arbitrary in their definitions. Indeed, they must still be used, for
want of a more modern system of notation,
when the legitimacy of a line has to be tested;
for, after all, the English "licentiate iambic"
has a form, although the deflections from that
form constitute its beauties. I only contend
that it is impossible to apply with rigour rules
deduced from the analysis of quantitative
metres, to versification based upon accent and
emphasis; and also that when such application
has been made, and the scansion has been
determined, we have still to seek the æsthetic
value of the lines in question. It may, of
course, be answered that the same difficulty
meets us in classic poetry — that the finest
passages of Æschylus and Virgil do not owe
their beauty to their scansion, and that in
reading them we habitually ignore it.* That
is true; but it is none the less true that they

* The matter is further complicated by the fact that we are
quite ignorant how the Greeks read their verse, and that we
are not quite sure about the pronunciation of Latin.

strictly obey the rules of quantitative scansion, whereas it cannot be proved that our Blank Verse is bound by the like limitations. This constitutes a decisive difference; and the obstinate search for quantitative scansion, even when we have agreed to substitute accents for proper longs and shorts, leads to such misconceptions of the genius of Blank Verse as rendered Johnson's essay on the versification of Milton ridiculous.

The remarks expressed in the foregoing paragraphs, together with the two following studies on the history and the mechanism of Blank Verse, are not published without misgivings. The whole subject of metre is so complex, so entangled with questions of pronunciation, elocution, musical analogy, and proportional values of concatenated syllables varying in the case of each language, yet probably capable of being scientifically reduced to simple rules under laws as yet but dimly apprehended, that a prudent critic might well hesitate before exposing his crude speculations to the world.* The conviction that as yet no congruity of doctrine has been arrived at—that we are still forced to adapt the nomenclature of a prosody deduced from the analysis of the most highly perfected Greek metres to rhythmical systems based on different principles — that we have not sufficiently distinguished between the metrical substratum and the æsthetical or rhetorical effect — induces me to court censure, in the hope that further progress may be made in a region where each observer is apt to tax his fellow-workers with a want of intelligence. The best craftsmen work by instinct, and the subtlest *dilettanti* of their masterpieces are contented with sensation. It still remains for the analyst to discover the laws which have regulated the artistic instinct in the production of exquisitely pleasurable combinations.

* As instances of these difficulties, I might point out the choice of hendecasyllabic iambic lines by the Italians, and the loose structure of the French Alexandrine, which seems to defy scansion, depending on cæsura, pause, and rhyme.

II

THE HISTORY OF BLANK VERSE

ENGLISH blank verse is, perhaps, more various and plastic than any other national metre. It is capable of being used for the most commonplace and the most sublime utterances ; so that, without any alteration in the vehicle, we pass from merely colloquial dialogue to strains of impassioned soliloquy, from comic repartee to tragic eloquence, from terse epigrams to elaborate descriptions. Originally instituted for the drama, it received in Milton's hands an epical treatment, and has by authors of our own day been used for idyllic, and even for lyrical compositions. Yet all of these so widely different applications have only served to develop, without exhausting its resources. Plato mentions a Greek musical instrument

16

called panharmonion, which was adapted to express the different modes and systems of melodious utterance. This name might be applied to our blank verse; there is no harmony of sound, no dignity of movement, no swiftness, no subtlety of languid sweetness, no brevity, no force of emphasis beyond its scope. In hearing good blank verse, we do not long for rhyme; our ears are satisfied without it; nor does our sense of order and proportion require the obvious and artificial recurrence of stanzas, when the sense creates for itself a melodious structure, and is not forced into the mould of any arbitrary form. So much can hardly be said for any other metre. The Greeks, who were peculiarly sensitive to self-imposed canons of fitness in art, reserved the hexameter for epical and idyllic poetry, the iambic for satire and the drama, the elegiac for inscriptions, epigrams, and minor compositions of a more personal character, and other complex structures for lyrical and choral utterances. To have written an

epic or an idyll in iambics would to them have
seemed inexcusable. And for this reason, the
iambic was limited both in its use and its
development. Two sorts were recognised—
the one adapted to the loose and flowing style
of comic conversation; the other to the more
ceremonious and measured march of tragic
dialogue and description. But when the
action of the play became animated, instead
of accelerating the iambic rhythm, the poet
used trochaic or anapæstic measures, obeying
the law of variety by adopting a new mode
externally fitted to express the change he had
in view.

In the infancy of our drama, rhyme, as the
natural accompaniment of mediæval poetry,
had universally been used, until the courtiers
of Elizabeth bethought them of inventing
some more solemn and stately metre in imitation of the classic. It will be remembered
that attempts to naturalise Greek and Roman
rhythms in our language were then fashion-
able. Sidney and the *literati* of the *Areo-*

pagus spent their leisure hours in fashioning
uncouth hexameters ; and Roger Ascham,
though he recognised the incapacity of English for scansion, was inclined to welcome
an unrhymed metre like the classical iambic.
Surrey first solved the problem practically by
translating parts of the " Æneid" into verses
of ten syllables without rhyme. But his
measure has not much variety or ease. It
remained for two devoted admirers of classical
art, Sackville and Norton, to employ what
Surrey called his " strange metre " in the
drama. Their " Gorboduc," acted before the
Queen in 1561-2, is the first tragedy written
in blank verse. The insufferable monotony
and dreariness of this play are well known
to all students of our early literature. Yet
respect for its antiquity induces me to give a
specimen of its quaint style. We must remember in reading these lines that they are
the embryon of Marlowe's, Shakspere's, and
Milton's verse.

O mother, thou to murder thus thy child!
Even Jove with justice must with lightning flames
From heaven send down some strange revenge on thee.
Ah, noble prince, how oft have I beheld
Thee mounted on thy fierce and trampling steed,
Shining in armour bright before the tilt,
And with thy mistress' sleeve tied on thy helm,
And charge thy staff—to please thy lady's eye—
That bowed the headpiece of thy friendly foe!

I have purposely chosen the most animated apostrophe in the whole play, in order that its venerable authors might appear to the best advantage. It will be noticed that notwithstanding much stiffness in the movement of the metre, and some embarrassment in the grammatical construction, we yet may trace variety and emphasis in the pauses of these lines beyond what would at that epoch have been possible in sequences of rhymed couplets. Mr. Collier, in his "History of Dramatic Poetry," mentions two other plays written in blank verse, but not performed on the public stage, before the appearance of Marlowe's "Tamburlaine." It is to this tragedy that he assigns the credit of having once and for all

established blank verse as the popular dramatic
metre of the English. With this opinion all
students who have examined the origin of our
theatrical literature will, no doubt, agree. But
Marlowe did not merely drive the rhymed
couplet from the stage by substituting the
blank verse of his contemporaries : he created
a new metre by the melody, variety, and force
which he infused into the iambic, and left
models of versification, the pomp of which
Shakspere and Milton alone can be said
to have surpassed. The change which he
operated was so thorough and so novel to the
playwrights as well as the playgoers of his
time, that he met with some determined opposition. Thomas Nash spoke scornfully of
" idiot art masters, that intrude themselves to
our ears as the alchemists of eloquence, who
(mounted on the stage of eloquence) think to
attract better pens with the swelling bombast
of bragging blank verse." In another sneer
he described the new measure as " the spacious
volubility of a drumming decasyllabon;" while

Robert Greene, who had written many wearisome rhymed dramas, talked of making "verse jet on the stage in tragical buskins, every word filling the ear like the fa-burden of Bow bell, daring God out of heaven with that atheist Tamburlan, or blaspheming with the mad priest of the Sun." But our "licentiate iambic" was destined to triumph. Greene and Nash gave way before inevitable fate, and wrote some better plays in consequence.

Let us inquire what change Marlowe really introduced, and what was his theory of dramatic versification. He found the ten-syllabled heroic line monotonous, monosyllabic and divided into five feet of tolerably regular alternate short and long. He left it various in form and structure, sometimes redundant by a syllable, sometimes deficient, enriched with unexpected emphases and changes in the beat. He found no sequence or attempt at periods; one line succeeded another with insipid regularity, and all were made after the same model. He grouped his verse according to the sense, obeying an internal law of melody, and allowing the thought contained in his words to dominate their form. He did not force his metre to preserve a fixed and unalterable type, but suffered it to assume most variable modulations, the whole beauty of which depended upon their perfect adaptation to the current of his ideas. By these means he was able to produce the double effect of variety and unity, to preserve the fixed march of his chosen metre, and yet, by subtle alterations in the pauses, speed and grouping of the syllables, to make one measure represent a thousand. Used in this fashion, blank verse became a Proteus. It resembled music, which requires regular time and rhythm ; but, by the employment of phrase, induces a higher kind of melody to rise above the common and despotic beat of time. Bad writers of blank verse, like Marlowe's predecessors, or like those who in all ages have been deficient in plastic energy and power of harmonious modulation, produce successions of monotonous iambic lines, sacrificing the poetry of expression to the mechanism of their art. Metre with them ceases to be the organic body of a vital thought, and becomes a mere framework. And bad critics praise them for the very faults of tameness and monotony which they miscall regularity of numbers. It was thus that the sublimest as well as the most audacious of Milton's essays in versification fell under the censure of Johnson.

It is not difficult to support these eulogies by reference to Marlowe's works; for some of his finest blank verse passages allow themselves to be detached without any great injury to their integrity. The following may be cited as an instance of his full-voiced harmony. Faustus exclaims:

> Have I not made blind Homer sing to me
> Of Alexander's love and Œnon's death ?
> And hath not he who built the walls of Troy
> With ravishing sound of his melodious harp
> Made music with my Mephistophiles ?

We feel at once that a new spirit has been breathed into the metre—a spirit of undefinable melody. Something is owing to the choice of long-resounding and full-vowelled words; something to the use of monosyllables, as in the third line; something to alliteration; but more than all to the passion of the author, and to the "plastic stress" of his creative genius. This tragedy is full of fine passages, and the soliloquy in which Faustus watches his last moments ebb away, might be quoted as a perfect instance of variety and sustained effect in a situation which could only be redeemed from monotony by consummate art. "Edward the Second" is not less rich in versification. In order to prove that Marlowe could temper his blank verse to different moods and passions, take this speech, in which the indignant Edward first gives way to anger, and then to misery:

> Mortimer! who talks of Mortimer,
> Who wounds me with the name of Mortimer,
> That bloody man? Good father, on thy lap
> Lay I this head laden with mickle care,
> O, might I never ope these eyes again,
> Never again lift up this drooping head,
> O, never more lift up this dying heart!

The didactic dignity of Marlowe's verse may be gathered from these lines in "Tamburlaine" :

> Our souls whose faculties can comprehend
> The wondrous architecture of the world,
> And measure every wandering planet's course,
> Still climbing after knowledge infinite,
> And always moving as the restless spheres,
> Will us to wear ourselves, and never rest
> Until we reach the ripest fruit of all,
> That perfect bliss and sole felicity,
> The sweet fruition of an earthly crown.

Again, as if wishing to prove what liberties might be taken with the iambic metre without injury to its music, Marlowe wrote these descriptive lines in the "Jew of Malta" :

> Bags of fiery opals, sapphires, amethysts,
> Jacinths, hard topaz, grass-green emeralds,
> Beauteous rubies, sparkling diamonds,
> And seld seen costly stones of so great price,
> As one of them, indifferently rated,
> May serve, in peril of calamity,
> To ransom great kings from captivity.

The licence of the first and third line is both daring and successful. The second departs less from the ordinary rhythm, while the four last carry back the period into the usual flow of Marlowe's verse.

The four passages which I have quoted are, perhaps, sufficient to prove that blank verse was not only brought into existence, but also perfected by Marlowe. It is true that, like all great poets, he left his own peculiar imprint on it, and that his metre is marked by an almost extravagant exuberance, impetuosity, and height of colouring. It seems to flow from him with the rapidity of improvisation, and to follow a law of melody rather felt than studied by its author. We feel that the poet loved to give the rein to his ungovernable fancy, forgetting the thought with which he started, revelling in sonorous words, and pouring forth a stream of images, so that the mind receives at last a vague and various impression of sublimity.

Marlowe's contemporaries soon caught the trick of sonorous versification. The obscure author of a play which has sometimes been attributed to Marlowe, wrote these lines in the true style of his master :

> Chime out your softest strains of harmony,
> And on delicious music's silken wings
> Send ravishing delight to my love's ears.

Peele contented himself with repeating his more honeyed cadences.

Shakspere, next to Marlowe, had more influence than any poet on the formation of our blank verse. Coleridge has maintained that his diction and metre were peculiarly his own, unimitated and inimitable. But I believe that a careful comparison of his style with that of his contemporaries will make it evident that he began a period in which versification was refined and purified from Marlowe's wordiness. Shakspere has more than Marlowe's versatility and power ; but his metre is never so extravagant in its pomp of verbal grandeur. He restrains his own luxuriance, and does not allow himself to be seduced by pleasing sounds. His finest passages owe none of their beauty to alliteration, and yet he knew most exquisitely how to use that meretricious handmaid of melody. Nothing can be more seductive than the charm of repeated liquids and vowels in the following lines :

> On such a night
> Stood Dido with a willow in her hand
> Upon the wild sea banks and waft her love
> To come again to Carthage.

Nor again did Shakspere employ big sounding words so profusely as Marlowe, but reserved them for effects of especial solemnity, as in the speech of Timon :

> Come not to me again : but say to Athens,
> Timon hath made his everlasting mansion
> Upon the beachèd verge of the salt flood ;
> Whom once a day with his embossèd froth
> The turbulent surge shall cover; thither come,
> And let my gravestone be your oracle.

But Shakspere did not always, or indeed often, employ these somewhat obvious artifices of harmonious diction. The characteristic of his verse is that it is naturally, unobtrusively, and enduringly musical. We hardly know why his words are melodious, or what makes them always fresh, whereas the more apparent charms of Fletcher and of Marlowe pall upon our ears. Throughout his writings there is a subtle adjustment of sound to sense, of lofty thoughts to appropriate words; the ideas evolve themselves with inexhaustible spontaneity, and a suitable investiture of language is never wanting, so that each cadenced period seems made to hold a thought of its own, and thought is linked to thought and cadence to cadence in unending continuity. Inferior artists have systems of melody, pauses which they repeat, favourite terminations, and accelerations or retardations of the rhythm, which they employ whenever the occasion prompts them. But there is none of this in Shakspere. He never falls into the commonplace of mannerism. Compare Oberon's speeches with Prospero's, or with Lorenzo's, or with Romeo's, or with Mark Antony's; under the Shaksperian similarity there is a different note in all of these, whereas we know beforehand what form the utterances of

BLANK VERSE

Bellario, or Philaster, or Memnon, or Ordella in Fletcher must certainly assume. As a single instance of the elasticity, self-restraint, and freshness of the Shaksperian blank verse; of its freedom from Marlowe's turgidity, or Fletcher's languor, or Milton's involution; of its ringing sound and lucid vigour, the following celebrated passage from "Measure for Measure" may be quoted. It illustrates the freedom from adventitious ornament and the organic continuity of Shakspere's versification, while it also exhibits his power of varying his cadences and suiting them to the dramatic utterance of his characters.

> Ay, but to die, and go we know not where;
> To lie in cold obstruction and to rot;
> This sensible warm motion to become
> A kneaded clod; and the delighted spirit
> To bathe in fiery floods, or to reside
> In thrilling regions of thick ribbed ice;
> To be imprisoned in the viewless winds,
> And blown with restless violence about
> The pendant world; or to be worse than worst
> Of those that lawless and incertain thoughts
> Imagine howling;—'tis too horrible!
> The weariest and most loathed worldly life,

That age, ache, penury, and imprisonment
Can lay on Nature, is a paradise
To what we fear of death.

Each of Shakspere's contemporaries and successors among the dramatists commanded a style of his own in blank verse composition. It was so peculiarly the function of the stage and of the playwrights at that particular epoch to perfect this metre, that I do not think some detailed examination of the language of the drama will be out of place. Coleridge observes that " Ben Jonson's blank verse is very masterly and individual." To this criticism might be added that it is the blank verse of a scholar—pointed, polished, and free from the lyricisms of his age. It lacks harmony and is often laboured : but vigorous and solid it never fails to be. This panegyric of poetry from the Italianised version of " Every Man in his Humour," may be taken as a specimen of his most animated style :

I can repel opinion and approve
The state of poesy, such as it is,
Blessed, eternal, and most true divine ;
Indeed, if you will look on poesy,

As she appears in many, poor and lame,
Patched up in remnants and old worn-out rags,
Half starved for want of her peculiar food,
Sacred invention; then I must confess
Both your conceit and censure of her merit:
But view her in her glorious ornaments,
Attired in the majesty of art,
Set high in spirit with the precious taste
Of sweet philosophy; and which is most,
Crowned with the rich traditions of a soul
That hates to have her dignity profaned
With any relish of an earthly thought—
Oh! then how proud a presence doth she bear!
Then she is like herself, fit to be seen
Of none but grave and consecrated eyes.

After a complete perusal of his works I find very little of the fluent grace which belonged in so large a measure to Fletcher and to Shakspere. Yet the first lines of the "Sad Shepherd" have a very delicate music; they are almost unique in Ben Jonson:

Here was she wont to go! and here! and here!
Just where these daisies, pinks, and violets grow:
The world may find the spring by following her;
For other print her airy steps ne'er left.
Her treading would not bend a blade of grass,
Or shake the downy blue bell from his stalk!
But like the soft west wind she shot along,
And where she went, the flowers took thickest root,
As she had sowed them with her odorous foot.

The melody which gives so chaste and elegant
a beauty to these lines is invariable in the
verse of Beaumont and Fletcher. We have
too much of it there, and surfeit on sweets; for
in a very short time we discover the trick of
these great versifiers and learn to expect their
luxurious alliterations, and repeated cæsuras at
the end of the fifth syllable. Their redundant
and deficient lines, the sweetness long drawn
out of their delicious cadences, become well
known. Then the movement of their verse is
not, like that of Shakspere, self-evolved and
thoroughly organic; it obeys a rule; luxury is
sought for its own sake, and languor follows
as a direct consequence of certain verbal man-
nerisms. Among these may be mentioned a
decided preference for all words in which there
is a predominance of liquids and of vowels.
For instance, in this line:

> Showers, hails, snows, frosts, and two-edged winds that prime
> The maiden blossoms,

there is no unlicensed redundancy of syllables;
but the labour of getting through so many

accumulated sounds produces a strange retardation of the movement. Another peculiarity is the substitution of hendecasyllabic lines for the usual decasyllable blank verse through long periods of dialogue. In one scene of "Valentinian" there are fifty-five continuous lines, of which only five are decasyllabic verses, the rest being hendecasyllables; so that the licence of the superfluous syllable, which is always granted in dramatic writing for the sake of variety, becomes, in its turn, far more cloying than a strict adherence to the five-footed verse. It is also noticeable that this weak ending is frequently constructed by the addition of some emphatic monosyllable. Thus:

> I do remember him; he was my guardian,
> Appointed by the senate to preserve me:
> What a full majesty sits in his face yet.

Or:

> The desolations that this great eclipse works.

The natural consequence of these delays and languors in the rhythm is that the versification of Beaumont and Fletcher has always a meandering and rotary movement. It does

not seem to leap or glide straight onward,
but to return upon itself and wind and double.
The following passage may be quoted as illustrative of its almost lyrical voluptuousness:

> I do her wrong, much wrong: she's young and blessed,
> Fair as the spring, and as his blossoms tender;
> But I a nipping North-wind, my head hung
> With hails and frosty icicles: are the souls so too
> When they depart hence, lame and old and loveless?
> Ah, no! 'tis ever youth there: Age and Death
> Follow our flesh no more, and that forced opinion
> That spirits have no sexes, I believe not.

The speech of Aspatia among her maidens
is an excellent example of the more careful
verse of Fletcher:

> Fie, you have missed it here, Antiphila,
> You are much mistaken, wench;
> These colours are not dull and pale enough,
> To show a soul so full of misery
> As this sad lady's was; do it by me,
> Do it again by me the lost Aspatia,
> And you shall find all true but the wild island.
> I stand upon the sea beach now, and think
> Mine arms thus, and mine hair blown with the wind,
> Wild as that desert, and let all about me
> Tell that I am forsaken; do my face
> (If thou hadst ever feeling of a sorrow,)
> Thus, thus, Antiphila, strive to make me look
> Like Sorrow's monument; and the trees about me,
> Let them be dry and leafless; let the rocks

Groan with continual surges, and behind me
Make all a desolation ; look, look, wenches,
A miserable life of this poor picture !

There is enough variety and subtle melody in this without the usual effeminacy of Fletcher's style. Whatever makes it most effective is that it is written so as to represent the natural inflections of tone, the pauses, and the emphases of the character who speaks it. One more specimen of this most musical of poets may be allowed me. It is from "Thierry and Theodoret." Thierry speaks and Ordella answers :

Th. 'Tis full of fearful shadows.
Ord.   So is sleep, sir,
Or any thing that's merely ours and mortal ;
We were begotten gods else : but these fears,
Feeling but once the fires of noble thoughts,
Fly, like the shapes of clouds we form, to nothing.
Th. Suppose it death.
Ord. I do.
Th.   And endless parting
With all we can call ours, with all our sweetness,
With youth, strength, pleasure, people, time, nay
    reason.
For in the silent grave no conversation,
No joyful tread of friends, no voice of lovers,
No careful father's counsel ; nothing's heard,
Nor nothing is, but all oblivion,

> Dust, and an endless darkness, and dare you, woman,
> Desire this place?
> *Ord.* 'Tis of all sleeps the sweetest;
> Children begin it to us, strong men seek it,
> And kings from height of all their painted glories
> Fall like spent exhalations to this centre.

There the poet should have stopped, for exquisite thoughts have hitherto been rendered in exquisite language. He continues, however, for five lines of inferior beauty.

Turning from the more celebrated to the less distinguished playwrights, we find almost universally the power of writing forcible blank verse. Marston condensed much thought into his lines, and made such epigrams as these:

> Can man by no means creep out of himself
> And leave the slough of viperous grief behind?

or such addresses of concentrated passion as this prologue:

> Therefore we proclaim
> If any spirit breathes within this round,
> Uncapable of weighty passion
> (As from his birth being hugged in the arms
> And nuzzled 'twixt the breasts of Happiness),
> Who winks and shuts his apprehension up
> From common sense of what men were, and are;
> Who would not know what men must be: let such
> Hurry amain from our black-visaged shows;

> We shall afright their eyes. But if a breast,
> Nailed to the earth with grief, if any heart,
> Pierced through with anguish, pant within this ring;
> If there be any blood whose heat is choked
> And stifled with true sense of misery—
> If aught of these strains fill this consort up—
> They do arrive most welcome.

We find both quaintness of language and roughness of rhythm in these lines ; but how weighty, how eloquently solemn, is the apostrophe to those of the spectators whose own sorrows render them participant of tragic woes. It is clear that a large and broad *style*, a sense of rhythm, and a freedom in the use of blank verse as a natural vehicle of thought, were epidemic in that age.

Facility for expressing every shade of sentiment or reflection in clear and simple lines belonged peculiarly to Decker, Heywood, Middleton, and Rowley, poets who made but little pretension to melodious charms and flowers of fancy, but whose native ear maintained such flowing periods as the following :

> *D.* Thy voice sends forth such music, that I never
> Was ravished with a more celestial sound.

Were every servant in the world like thee,
So full of goodness, angels would come down
To dwell with us. Thy name is Angelo,
And like that name thou art. Get thee to rest;
Thy youth with too much watching is oppressed.
A. No, my dear lady. I could weary stars,
And force the wakeful moon to lose her eyes,
By my late watching; but to wait on you,
When at your prayers you kneel before the altar,
Methinks I'm singing with some choir in heaven,
So blest I hold me in your company.
Therefore, my most loved mistress, do not bid
Your boy, so serviceable, to get hence;
For then you break his heart.

The same praise belongs to Massinger, who was, indeed, associated with Decker in the production of the play from which these lines are quoted. Coleridge remarks that he has reconciled the language of everyday life with poetical diction more thoroughly than any other writer of dramatic blank verse, and for this reason he recommends him as a better model for young writers than Shakspere, who is far too individual, and Fletcher, who is too monotonously lyrical.

If it is the case with all our dramatists that the melody of their versification depends entirely upon the sense of their words, this is particularly true of Massinger. It will be noticed that all the changes in his rhythm are accounted for by changes in the thought, or answer to supposed alterations of the actor's gestures and of his voice. In lighter moods, Massinger could use hendecasyllabic periods with much of Fletcher's melody. This is a specimen :

> Not far from where my father lives, a lady,
> A neighbour by, blest with as great a beauty
> As nature durst bestow without undoing,
> Dwelt, and most happily, as I thought then,
> And blessed the house a thousand times she dwelt in.
> This beauty, in the blossom of my youth,
> When my first fire knew no adulterate incense,
> Nor I no way to flatter but my fondness,
> In all the bravery my friends could show me,
> In all the faith my innocence could give me,
> In the best language my true tongue could tell me,
> And all the broken sighs my sick heart lent me,
> I sued and served. Long did I love this lady,
> Long was my travail, long my trade, to win her ;
> With all the duty of my soul I served her.

There is no need to call attention to the alliterative structures of this period. They are strongly marked. Massinger represents a whole class of the later Elizabethan play-

wrights, who used a flowing blank verse, perfected by long practice for the purpose of the
stage. Shirley was one of this set; he wrote
evenly and with due attention to the meaning
of his words. But there were other ambitious
versifiers, like Ford, who sought for more
recondite and elaborate graces. It has been
thought that Ford imitated Shakspere in his
style as much as in the situations of his
dramas. I cannot myself perceive much trace
of Shakspere in the verse of Ford; but these
two specimens will enable the reader to judge
fairly of his rhetoric :

Hie to thy father's house, there lock thee fast
Alone within thy chamber; then fall down
On both thy knees, and grovel on the ground;
Cry to thy heart, wash every word thou utterest
In tears, and (if 't be possible) of blood :
Beg heaven to cleanse the leprosy of lust
That rots thy soul; acknowledge what thou art,
A wretch, a worm, a nothing : weep, sigh, pray
Three times a day, and three times every night;
For seven days' space do this; then, if thou findest
No change in thy desires, return to me,
I'll think on remedy. Pray for thyself
At home, whilst I pray for thee here; away—
My blessing with thee—we have need to pray.

The lines are much more broken up than is usual with our dramatists. They sparkle with short sentences and quick successions of reiterated sounds. The same effect is noticeable in Calantha's dying speech, where the situation is quite different :

> Forgive me. Now I turn to thee, thou shadow
> Of my contracted lord : bear witness all,
> I put my mother's wedding-ring upon
> His finger; 'twas my father's last bequest :
> Thus I now marry him whose wife I am!
> Death shall not separate us. O, my lords,
> I but deceived your eyes with antic gesture,
> When one news straight came huddling on another,
> Of death, and death, and death; still I danced forward.
> But it struck home, and here, and in an instant.
> Be such mere women, who with shrieks and outcries,
> Can vow a present end to all their sorrows ;
> Yet live to vow new pleasures, and outlive them.
> They are the silent griefs which cut the heart strings ;
> Let me die smiling.

This is a sculptured and incisive style. Even the largo (to borrow a term from music) of Calantha's address to her nobles, though it assumes hendecasyllabic stateliness, maintains the crisp and pointed motion of the lines that had preceded it. While speaking of Ben

Jonson or of Marston would have been the
proper time to mention the blank verse of
George Chapman, a very manly and scholar-
like author. He expressed philosophical ideas
in elevated language. This eulogy of honour-
able love is vigorous in thought as well as
metre :

> 'Tis nature's second sun,
> Causing a spring of virtues where he shines ;
> And as without the sun, the world's great eye,
> All colours, beauties, both of art and nature,
> Are given in vain to man; so without love
> All beauties bred in women are in vain,
> All virtues born in men lie buried ;
> For love informs them as the sun doth colours ;
> And as the sun, reflecting his warm beams
> Against the earth, begets all fruits and flowers,
> So love, fair shining in the inward man,
> Brings forth in him the honourable fruits
> Of valour, wit, virtue, and haughty thoughts,
> Brave resolution, and divine discourse.

There is nothing in this passage which can be
termed highly poetical. It is chiefly interest-
ing as showing the plasticity of language and
of metre in the hands of our Elizabethan
authors. They fixed their minds upon their
thoughts, as we should do in writing prose,

and turned out terse and pregnant lines not unadorned with melody.

I have hitherto purposely abstained from speaking about Webster, a poet of no ordinary power, whose treatment of blank verse is specially illustrative of all the licences which were permitted by the playwrights of that time. His language is remarkably condensed, elliptical, and even crabbed. His verse is broken up into strange blocks and masses, often reading like rhythmical prose. It is hard, for instance, to make a five-footed line out of the following :

> To be executed again ; who must despatch me ?

Yet close analysis will always prove that there was method in the aberrations of Webster, and that he used his metre as the most delicate and responsive instrument for all varieties of dramatic expression. Avoiding the sing-song of Greene and Peel, the lyrical sweetness of Fletcher, the prosaic gravity of Jonson, the limpid fluency of Heywood and Decker, the tumid magniloquence of Marlowe, and the glittering regularity of Ford, he perfected a style which depends for its effect upon the emphases and pauses of the reciter. One of the most striking lines in his tragedy of the " Duchess of Malfi " proves how boldly and how successfully Webster sacrificed metre to expression. A brother is looking for the first time after death on the form of a sister whom he has caused to be murdered :

Cover her face ; mine eyes dazzle ; she died young.

There is no cæsura, no regular flow of verse, in this line, though in point of syllables it is not more redundant than half of Fletcher's. Each sentence has to be said separately, with long intervals and sighs, that indicate the working of remorseful thought. The powerful collocation of his words may be illustrated by such a line as :

Other sins only speak ; murder shrieks out !

where the logical meaning can hardly fail to be emphasised by the reader. Scansion in the verse of Webster is subordinate to the purpose of the speaker; in writing it he no doubt imagined his actors declaiming with great variety of intonation, with frequent and lengthy pauses, and with considerable differences in the rapidity of their utterances. The dialogue of the duchess with her waiting-maid on the subject of the other world and death is among the finest for its thoughts and language. As far as rhythm contributes to its excellences, they depend entirely upon the pauses, emphases, and irregularities of all sorts which are used. The duchess begins :

> O, that it were possible we might
> But hold some two days' conference with the dead.
> From them I should learn somewhat, I am sure,
> I never shall know here.

Up to this point the verses have run smoothly for Webster. But the duchess has exhausted one vein of meditation. Her voice sinks, and she falls into a profound reverie. When she rouses herself again to address Cariola, she starts with a new thought, and the line is made redundant :

BLANK VERSE

> I'll tell thee a miracle;
> I am not mad yet to my cause of sorrow:
> The heaven o'er my head seems made of molten brass,
> The earth of flaming sulphur; yet I am not mad.

To eke out the second line the voice is made to dwell with emphasis upon the word " mad," while the third and fourth have each twelve syllables, which must be pronounced with desperate energy and distinctness—as it were rapidly beneath the breath. But again her passion changes. It relents, and becomes more tender. And for a space we have verses that flow more evenly:

> I am acquainted with sad misery;
> As the tanned galley-slave is with his oar;
> Necessity makes me suffer constantly,
> And custom makes it easy.

At this point she sinks into meditation, and on rousing herself again with a fresh thought, the verse is broken and redundant:

> What do I look like now?

Cariola answers plainly, and her lines have a smooth rhythm:

Like to your picture in the gallery,
A deal of life in show, but none in practice ;
Or rather like some reverend monument,
Whose ruins are even pitied.

The duchess takes up this thought :

Very proper ;
And fortune seems only to have her eyesight
To behold my tragedy.

Here her contemplation is broken by the
approach of a messenger, and she exclaims,
without completing the line :

How now ?
What noise is that ?

It might seem almost hypercritical to remark,
that when the train of thought is broken from
without, the verse is deficient ; when broken
by the natural course of the speaker's reflection, it is redundant. Yet this may be
observed in the instances which I have quoted,
and there is a real reason for it. The redundant line indicates the incubation of long-
continued reverie ; the deficient very well
expresses that short and sudden cessation of
thought which is produced by an interruption
from without. The remarks which I have

made on Webster's style apply with almost
equal force to that of his contemporaries. We
read in " Hamlet," for instance :

> This bodily creation ecstasy
> Is very cunning in.
>   Ecstasy !

The second line is defective in one syllable.
That syllable, to Shakspere's delicate sense of
the value of sounds and pauses, was supplied
by Hamlet's manner. The prince was meant,
no doubt, to startle his audience by the sudden
repetition of the word "ecstasy," after a quick
gesture of astonishment.

To those who read the pages of our
dramatists with this conception of their metre,
its irregularities furnish an unerring index to
the inflections which the actors must have used,
to the characters which the poets designed, and
to the situations which they calculated. The
want of action is thus in some measure com-
pensated, and it becomes apparent that the
true secret of blank verse consists in the proper
adaptation of words and rhythms to the sense

contained in them. On this point I have already more than once insisted. I repeat it because it seems to me that blank verse cannot be properly appreciated, far less properly written, unless it be remembered that thought must always run before expression, and mould language to its own particular uses. Blank verse is indeed a sort of divinised prose. Unlimited by rhyme or stanza, it has the freedom of *oratio soluta* subject to severe laws of rhythm. In the cunning use of this liberty, in the continual creation of melodious form adapted to the ever-varying subtleties of thought and feeling, lies the secret of the versifier's art.

Having traced the origin and development of blank verse upon the stage, and seen the congruence of liberty and law, the harmony of thought and form, which constitutes its beauty, we can understand how Milton came to use it as he did. Milton was deeply read in the Elizabethan authors; he profited by all of them and wore their mantle with a double portion of their power. Nor did he fail to feel the necessity of raising this metre, without altering its essential nature, to the epical dignity of the Virgilian hexameter; so that he added structures of more complex melody than had been used upon the stage, periods more fitted to reading or to recitation than to the rapid utterance of acted character. Yet, while he dignified the metre by epical additions, he never forgot that he was handling the verse of tragedy; and every one of the "remarkably unharmonious" lines which Johnson has collected in his essay on the versification of Milton, was not fashioned, as the critic hints, in slovenly haste, or in despair of making modern language musical, but was deliberately written in obedience to the highest laws of the metre which Marlowe, Shakspere, Fletcher, Webster, and the other dramatists had used. In suiting blank verse to epic poetry, Milton preserved the elasticity and force with which his predecessors had wielded it; his so-called harshness resulted from a deliberate or instinctive obedience to the genius of the English tragic metre. It seems hardly necessary to insist upon this view of Milton's versification. Yet the pernicious canons of the eighteenth century, when taste had become habituated to the mechanical regularity and meaningless monotony of the couplet, still prevail, and there are people who cannot read Milton by the sense and by their ear, but who cling blindly to the laws of rigorous scansion. A dispute arose some time ago in one of our leading papers, as to the proper reading of two lines in "Samson Agonistes;" where, by the way, dramatic licence was, to say the least, allowable. The lines run thus :

> Yet God hath wrought things as incredible
> For his people of old : what hinders now ?

It was suggested that they might be reduced to order by this transposition :

> Yet God of old hath for his people wrought
> Things as incredible : what hinders now ?

It is clear that the versification according to the second reading is far smoother. But is it

more Miltonic, and would it not be very easy
by a similar process of transposition to emas-
culate some of the most vigorous periods in
Milton's poetry, and to reduce his music to the
five-footed monotony of incompetent versifiers ? The truth is, that the chorus—or
Milton, who speaks in the chorus—does not
think about iambic regularity, but is intent on
arguing with Manoah. Its words of faith and
confidence rush forth :

> Yet God hath wrought things as incredible
> For his people of old——

then stop ; and the question follows after a
pause :

> What hinders now ?

Energy of meaning is thus communicated to
the double purpose of their argument. The
action of the speech is weakened by the suggested emendation. Take again line 175 of
" Samson Agonistes " :

> Universally crowned with highest praises,

and write it :

> Crowned universally with highest praises.

The first form is anomalous ; the second makes a very decent hendecasyllabic. Johnson, Bentley, and the like, would rejoice in so manipulating a hundred characteristic passages ; but true criticism looks backward and deduces its grounds of judgment from the predecessors rather than the successors of a poet. Adopting this standard, we should try Milton by Elizabethan models and not by the versifiers of the eighteenth century.

But these examples are taken from a tragedy. In "Paradise Lost" we find that Milton has varied the dramatic rhythm by a very sparing use of hendecasyllable lines and by introducing far more involved and artificial cadences. In fact the flow of epical language is naturally more sedate and complex than that of the drama ; for it has to follow the thoughts of one mind through all its reasonings. Yet the dramatic genius of the metre is for ever asserting itself, as in the following lines :

> Rejoicing but with awe,
> In adoration at his feet I fell
> Submiss; he reared me, and, " Whom thou soughtest
>   I am,"
> Said mildly, " Author of all this thou seest
> Above, or round about thee, or beneath."

Here if we fix our attention upon the lines and try to scan them, we find the third most dissonant. But if we read them by the sense, and follow the grouping of the thoughts, we terminate one cadence at " submiss," and after a moment of parenthetical description begin another period, which extends itself through the concluding lines. To analyse Miltonic blank verse in all its details would be the work of much study and prolonged labour. It is enough to indicate the fact that the most sonorous passages begin and end with interrupted lines, including in one organic structure, periods, parentheses, and paragraphs of fluent melody, that the harmonies are wrought by subtle and most complex alliterative systems, by delicate changes in the length and volume of syllables, and by the choice of names magnificent for their mere gorgeousness of sound. In these structures there are many pauses which enable the ear and voice to rest themselves, but none are perfect, none satisfy the want created by the opening hemistich, until the final and deliberate close is reached. Then the sense of harmony is gratified and we proceed with pleasure to a new and different sequence. If the truth of this remark is not confirmed by the following celebrated and essentially Miltonic passage, it must fall without further justification:

> And now his heart
> Distends with pride, and hardening in his strength,
> Glories; for never since created man
> Met such embodied force as named with these
> Could merit more than that small infantry
> Warred on by cranes: though all the giant brood
> Of Phlegra, with the heroic race were joined
> That fought at Thebes or Ilium, on each side
> Mixed with auxiliar Gods; and what resounds
> In fable or romance of Uther's son,
> Begirt with English and Armoric knights;
> And all who since, baptized or infidel,
> Jousted in Aspremont or Montalban,
> Damasco or Morocco or Trebizond,
> Or whom Biserta sent from Afric shore,
> When Charlemagne with all his peerage fell
> By Fontarabbia.

After perusing this quotation, let the reader compare it with Claudio's speech on Death in " Measure for Measure," and observe the difference between Shaksperian and Miltonic, between dramatic and epical blank verse. The one is simple in construction and progressive, the other is complex and stationary; but both are musical beyond the possibility of imitation. The one exhibits a thought, in the process of formation, developing itself from the excited fancy of the speaker. The other presents to us an image crystallised and perfect in the poet's mind; the one is in time, the other in space—the one is a growing and the other a complete organism. The whole difference between the drama and the epic is implicit in these periods. The one, if we may play upon a fancy, resembles Music, and the other Architecture.

In this again we find a proof that the structure of blank verse depends upon the nature of the thought which it is meant to clothe. The thoughts of a dramatist—whether his characters converse or soliloquise—are, of necessity, in evolution; the thoughts of an epical poet are before him, as matter which he must give form to. The richness and melody and variety of his versification will, in either case, depend upon the copiousness of his language, the delicacy of his ear, and the fertility of his invention. We owe everything to the nature of the poet, and very little to the decasyllables which he is using.

Milton was the last of the Elizabethans. With him the spirit of our literary renaissance became for the time extinct. Even during his lifetime the taste and capacity for blank verse composition had expired. It is said that Dryden wished to put "Paradise Lost" into couplets, and received from Milton the indifferent answer, "Let the young man tag his rhymes." Dryden, in his essay on dramatic poetry, defended the use of rhyme, and introduced the habit of writing plays in heroics, to the detriment of sense and character and freedom. Yet there are passages in his

later tragedies—" All for Love," "Cleopatra,"
" King Arthur," and " The Spanish Friar "—
which show that he could use the tragic metre
of blank verse with moderate ability. The
Elizabethan inspiration still feebly survives in
lines like these :

> The gods are just,
> But how can finite measure infinite ?
> Reason, alas ! it does not know itself !
> Yet man, vain man, will, with this short-lined plummet,
> Fathom the vast abyss of heavenly justice.
> Whatever is, is in its causes just,
> Since all things are by fate.   But purblind man
> Sees but a part of the chain, the nearest links ;
> His eyes not carrying to that equal beam
> That poises all above.

This is average thought expressed in average
words.   But " Absalom and Achitophel " is a
work of the very highest genius in its kind,
written not under the influence and inspiration
of age, but produced as the expression of a
different and no less genuine phase of national
development.   During the period of Dryden's
ascendency over English literature, very little
blank verse was written of much moment.

Yet, it must be remembered that the passage of the "Mourning Bride," which Johnson preferred to any single piece of English descriptive poetry, first saw the light in 1697. The lines begin—"How reverend is the face of this tall pile." They are dignified, melodious, and clear; but we already trace in the handling of the language more of the effort after neatness and precision, and less of Nature, than was common with the elder dramatists. After the death of Otway and Congreve, blank verse held the stage in the miserable compositions of the eighteenth century; but it had no true vitality. The real works of genius in that period were written in couplets, and it was not until the first dawn of a second renaissance in England, that blank verse began again to be practised. Meanwhile the use of the couplet had unfitted poets for its composition. Their acquired canons of regularity, when applied to loose and flowing metre, led them astray. They no longer trusted exclusively to their ear, but to a mechanism which rendered accuracy of ear almost useless, not to say impossible. Hence it followed, that when blank verse began again to be written, it found itself very much at the point where it had stood before the appearance of Marlowe. Even Thomson, who succeeded so well in imitating Spenserian stanza, wrote stiff and languid blank verse with monosyllabic terminations and monotonous cadences—a pedestrian style.

Cowper, in his translation of Homer, aimed at the Miltonic structure, and acquired a solemn though cumbrous versification. The description of the Russian empress's ice-palace, in " The Winter Morning Walk," proves how he had imbued himself with the language of the " Paradise Lost," and how naturally he adapted it to his own thoughts. Coleridge's blank verse has a kind of inflated grandeur, but not much of Elizabethan variety of music, subtlety of texture, and lightness of movement. His lines written in the Valley of Chamouni are sonorous ; but they want elasticity, and are inferior in quality to his lyrics. Heaviness of style and turgid rhetoric deface his verse and prose alike. Wordsworth again could not handle blank verse with any certainty of success. Wildernesses of the "Excursion" extend for pages and pages barren of beauty. We plod over them on foot, sinking knee-deep into the clinging sand; whereas the true master of blank verse carries us aloft as on a winged steed through cloud and sunshine in a yielding air. Wordsworth mistook the language of prose for that of Nature, and did not understand that natural verse might be written without the tedious heaviness of common disquisitions. One of his highest efforts is the poem on the Simplon Pass, introduced into the "Prelude." This owes its great beauty to the perfect delineation which he has succeeded in producing by suggestive images, by reiterated cadences, by solitary lines, by breathless repetitions, by the perfect union, in short, which subsists between the poet's mind and the nature he is representing.

Byron again is uncertain in his blank verse.

The lines on the Coliseum in " Manfred " are as good as a genuine Elizabethan passage, because they are spoken from the fulness of a poet's heart, and with a continuity of thought and copiousness of language which insured their organic vitality. But they are exceptional. Byron needed rhyme as an assistance to his defective melody. He did not feel that inner music which is the soul of true blank verse and sounding prose. In Keats at last we reach this power. His " Hyperion " is sung, not written, governed in all its parts by the controlling force of imagined melody. Its music is fluid, bound by no external measurement of feet, but determined by the sense and intonation of the poet's thought, while like the crotalos of the Athenian flute-player, the decasyllabic beat maintains an uninterrupted under-current of regular pulsations. Keats studied Milton and strove to imitate him. But he falls below the majesty and breadth of Milton's manner. He is too luxuriant in words and images, too loose in rhythm and prone to description. In fact, he produces an Elizabethan poem of even more wanton superfluity than those which he imitates. The entrance of Phœbus into his desecrated palace is a brilliant instance of the plasticity of language in a master's hand. But there is something florid in it which smacks of a degenerating taste in art. Some of Shelley's blank verse is perhaps the best which this century has produced, though it is too hasty and incoherent, especially in " Prometheus Unbound," to attain the equality of sustained style. In " Alastor " he shows what he can do both without imitation and by its help. The lines on Egypt are written with a true Miltonic roll and ponderous grandiloquence of aggregated names. But in the last paragraph of the poem we find the vernal freshness, elasticity, and delicacy that are Shelley's own. It is noticeable that both Keats and Shelley make an Elizabethan use of the so-called heroic couplet. " Epipsy-chidion " and " Lamia " are written, not in the metre of Dryden, Churchill, Pope, and Crabbe, but in that of Marlowe and Fletcher. Nothing proves more significantly the distance between the Elizabethan spirit and the taste of the eighteenth century, than the dissimilarity of these two metres, syllabically and in point of rhyme identical. The couplets of Marlowe, Fletcher, Shelley, and Keats, follow the laws of blank verse, and add rhyme—that is to say, their periods and pauses are entirely determined by the sense. The couplets of Dryden and his followers resemble Ovid's elegiacs in the permanence of their form and the restriction of their thought. Mr. Browning, who is one of the latest and most characteristic products of the Elizabethan revival, has made good use of this loose rhyming metre in "Sordello." Among the most melodious passages of that poem may be found the following :

You can believe
Sordello foremost in the regal class
Nature has broadly severed from the mass
Of men, and framed for pleasure, as she frames
Some happy lands that have luxurious names

For loose fertility ; a foot-fall there
Suffices to upturn to the warm air
Half germinating spices, mere decay
Produces richer life, and day by day
New pollen on the lily petal grows,
And still more labyrinthine buds the rose.

The whole structure of this period, in its pauses and studied disregard of the rhymed system, is that of blank verse. The final couplet completes the sense and satisfies the ear with regularity. Browning by fits and starts produces passages of fine blank verse, blowing out bubbles of magnificent sound as glass is blown from red-hot matter by the fierce breath and fiery will. Swinburne, when he chooses, sweeps the long purple, blows the golden trumpet, and intones the sacrificial chaunt of the Elizabethan hierarchy. He is a supreme artist in words; they obey him as the keys obey an organist, and from their combination he builds up melodious palaces of resonant magnificence. Tennyson must be named the most original and greatest living writer of blank verse. The classical beauty of the "Idylls of the King," the luxuriant eloquence of the "Princess," the calm majesty of "Ulysses," the idyllic sweetness of "Œnone," the grandeur of the "Mort d'Arthur," are monuments to the variety and scientific grasp of his genius. Subtle melody and self-restrained splendour are observable throughout his compositions. He has the power of selection and of criticism, the lack of which makes blank verse tumid or prosaic. It may be noticed that Tennyson has not only created for himself a style in narrative and descriptive blank verse, but that he has also adapted the Protean metre to lyrical purposes. Three songs in the "Princess," "Tears, idle tears," "Now sleeps the crimson petal," and "Come down, O maid," are perfect specimens of most melodious and complete minstrelsy in words. We observe that the first of these songs is divided into periods of five lines, each of which terminates with the words "days that are no more." This recurrence of sound and meaning is a substitute for rhyme, and suggests rhyme so persuasively that it is impossible to call the poem mere blank verse. The second song is less simple in its construction : it consists of a quatrain followed by three couplets, and succeeded by a final quatrain, each group of lines ending with the word "me." The lines are so managed, by recurrences of sound and by the restriction of the sense to separate lines, that the form of lyric verse is again imitated without aid of rhyme. Theocritus, in his Amœbean Idylls, had suggested this system ; and Shakspere, in the "Merchant of Venice" (act v. sc. 1), had shown what could be made of it in English. But the third song which I have mentioned depends for its effect upon no artificial structure, no reiterated sounds. The poet calls it an idyll : I think it may be referred to as a most convincing proof that the English language can be made perfectly lyrical and musical without the need of stanzas or of rhyme.

I have now passed in brief review the

greatest writers of blank verse, and have tried to show that this metre, originally formed for dramatic elocution, became epical, idyllic, lyrical, didactic, according to the will of the poets who made use of it. In conclusion, I may repeat some of the points which are established with reference to the scope and purpose of the metre. It seems adapted specially for thought in evolution; it requires progression and sustained effort. As a consequence of this, its melody is determined by the sense which it contains, and depends more upon proportion and harmony of sounds than upon recurrences and regularities of structure. This being its essential character, it follows that blank verse is better suited for dialogues, descriptions, eloquent appeals, rhetorical declamations, for all those forms of poetry which imply a continuity and development of thought, than for the setting forth of some one perfect and full-formed idea. The thought or "moment" which is sufficient for a sonnet would seem poor and fragmentary in fourteen lines of blank verse, unless they were distinctly understood to form a part of some continuous poem or dramatic dialogue. When, therefore, blank verse is used lyrically, the poet who manipulates it has to deceive the ear by structures analogous to those of rhymed stanzas. The harmony of our language is such as to admit of exquisite finish in this style; but blank verse sacrifices a portion of its characteristic freedom, and assimilates itself to another type of metrical expression, in the process. Another point about blank verse is that it admits of no mediocrity; it must be either clay or gold. Its writer gains no unreal advantage from the form of his versification, but has to produce fine thoughts in vigorous and musical language. Hence, we find that blank verse has been the metre of genius, that it is only used successfully by indubitable poets, and that it is no favourite in a mean, contracted, and unimaginative age. The freedom of the renaissance created it in England. The freedom of our century has reproduced it. Blank verse

BLANK VERSE

is a type and symbol of our national literary spirit—uncontrolled by precedent or rule, inclined to extravagance, yet reaching perfection at intervals by an inner force and *vivida vis* of native inspiration.

III

THE BLANK VERSE OF MILTON

AMONG the many points which connect the literature of this century with that of the Elizabethan age, there is none more marked and striking than the revival of a true feeling for the beauty of blank verse. Blank verse was the creation of our dramatists, from Marlowe to Massinger and Shirley, Milton received it at their hands ; but, in appropriating this metre to the Epic, even Milton thought it necessary to defend the use of unrhymed verse. Milton belonged by education and by disposition to the age which for want of a more accurate title has been called Elizabethan, but which may better be described as the Renaissance in England. That is to say, the spirit which gave form and life to our literature during the sixteenth and the first half of the seventeenth centuries, preserved its fullest vigour and manifested itself with the utmost splendour in the genius of Milton. But while he was yet alive, and by the publication of his masterpiece was proving his legitimate descent from the lineage of Spenser, Bacon, and Shakspere, a new and antagonistic spirit began to manifest itself. The poets and prose-writers of the Restoration stood no longer in a close relation to Italy and the classics, nor did they continue the tradition of the dramatists of our renaissance. They followed French examples, and introduced another standard of taste. One of the signs of this change was the rejection of blank verse, their exclusive practice of the couplet. To some extent this was a return to old English precedents, to the rhym-ing metre of Chaucer and the earliest English plays. But the heroic verse, as developed by Dryden, was not a regular continuation of the tradition handed down from Chaucer and from Marlowe. It had less in common with the metre of the "Canterbury Tale" and

"Hero and Leander" than with the French Alexandrine, and its adoption was one of the signs of the French influence which prevailed throughout the Restoration, and which determined the style of English literature for the following century.

The exchange of blank verse for the rhyming couplet was not so insignificant as at first sight it may appear. It was no mere whim of fashion or voluntary preference among the poets for one of two metres, either of which they could have used with equal mastery. On the contrary, it indicated a radical change in the spirit of our literature. With the substitution of heroic for unrhymed verse, the theory and practice of harmony in English composition were altered. What was essentially national in our poetry—the music of sustained periods, elastic in their structure, and governed by the subtlest laws of melody in recurring consonants and vowels—was sacrificed for the artificial eloquence and monotonous cadence of the couplet. For a century and a half the

summit of all excellence in versification was the
construction of neat pairs of lines, smooth
indeed and polished, but scarcely varying in
their form. The breadth and freedom of style,
the organic connection between thought and
rhythm, were abandoned for precise and
studied regularity ; and corresponding to this
restriction of the form and poetry was an
impoverishment in its matter both of thought
and fancy. The audacities of Shakspere and
the sublimities of Milton were no less unknown
and unappreciated than the volume and the
grandeur of their metrical effects. We might
compare this change in the spirit of our literature to the extinction of all the architectural
originality of the earlier Italian Renaissance
in the formal elegance of the Palladian
style. Of course it is not to be denied that
much was gained as well as lost. Not to speak
of the exaggerated conceits, fantastic phraseology, and faults of overstrained imagination,
which were eliminated in the age of the
Restoration and Queen Anne, it must always

be remembered that few literatures can exhibit
two types of excellence so great and yet so
diverse as those of our Elizabethan and
Classic periods. But the fact remains that
during this century and a half our authors
abandoned the fields in which the earliest and
most splendid laurels of the English had been
won, and our critics lost the sense for beauties
of style peculiarly national. To have written
true blank verse during the despotism of the
heroic couplet would have been impossible, and
to appreciate Shaksperian or Miltonic melody
was equally beyond the capacities of cultivated taste. It was not until the spirit of
the Elizabethan age revived in the authors of
the commencement of the present century that
blank verse began once more to be constructed
upon proper principles, and to be accepted at
its true value. Even then the habits of several
generations had to be laboriously broken, and
the metre which every playwright of the
sixteenth century commanded with facility was
used with pompous grandiosity or frigid

baldness, by poets even of distinguished genius.

These remarks serve merely as a preface to the following attempt to analyse the structure of Miltonic blank verse, and to explain some of the mistakes which have been made about it. Johnson's essay on the versification of Milton proves the want of intelligence which prevailed in the last century, and shows to what extent the exclusive practice of the couplet had spoiled the ears of critics for all the deeper and more subtle strains of which our language is capable. Johnson lays it down as a fixed canon that the English ten-syllable iambic measure is only pure and regular "when the accent rests upon every second syllable through the whole line." Thus such lines as these :

His constant lamp, and waves his purple wings . . . .
And mutual love, the crown of all our bliss, ...

which are not of very common occurrence in Milton, and perhaps are never met with in succession, he admits as pure; while all the others—those, that is to say, in which we recognise the triumphs of Miltonic art—he condemns as "more or less licentious with respect to accent." The tender and pathetic cadence of the last line in the following passage :

> This delicious place
> For us too large, where thy abundance wants
> Partakers, and uncropt falls to the ground,

is stigmatised by Johnson as remarkably inharmonious. Cowley's exquisite line :

> And the soft wings of peace cover him round.

which exhibits a similar cadence, meets with the same condemnation, Johnson adding magisterially, with reference to both examples : "In these the law of metre is very grossly violated by mingling combinations of sound directly opposite to each other, as Milton expresses it in his sonnet to Henry Lawes, by *committing short and long*, and setting one part of the measure at variance with the rest." Johnson's ear, accustomed to the sing-song of the couplet, and his instinct sophisticated by a too exclusive study of classical metres, exacted an even flow of regular iambics, which might occasionally be broken, for the sake of variety, by lines confessedly discordant. A superfluous syllable at rare intervals, or a trochee instead of an iamb in the first place, would be enough, he thought, to satisfy human weakness petulantly craving after change; then the metre should resume its calculated melody, and march on without interruption for a score or so of lines. But a trochee in the fourth place! (for so he scanned the lines), O Milton and Cowley! shame upon your ears! The ferule was raised, and down it came with a swinging blow upon the knuckles of the poets who had neglected their prosody. Johnson need not be followed through the details of his analysis. The canon already quoted is enough to prove how far he was from having discerned the true principles of criticism in this case. He attempted to reduce blank verse to rule by setting up the standard of an ideal line, any deviation whatever from which was to be called "licentious, impure, unharmonious," remaining ignorant the while that the whole effect of this metre depends upon the massing of lines in periods and on the variety of complicated cadences. Among other things, he had not perhaps considered that the fourth place in a ten-syllabled iambic is not the same as the fourth place in a line of twelve syllables.

Todd, commenting on Johnson's essay, shows a truer appreciation of Miltonic melody, and is properly indignant with the cool arrogance of Aristarchus. But he, too, is far from having perceived the laws which determine the structure of blank verse. After observing that "Milton was fond of the ancient measures," which indeed is true, he goes on to settle some of the lines that puzzled Johnson, thus: "These lines exhibit choriambics in the third and fourth, and in the fourth and fifth places:

For us too large, whēre thȳ ăbūndance wants
Partakers, and uncropt fālls tŏ thĕ grōund."

81   F

He thinks that he has answered Johnson and established something positive by his erudition *in re metricâ*, whereas he has only attained the negative result of demonstrating that blank verse must not be considered a mere sequence of iambi. It does not really satisfy any one to be told that two-fifths of each of these lines is what Horace might have called a choriambus, or that three-tenths of some other line is an anapæst. Johnson, to begin with, would not have been satisfied ; for he required iambi or their equivalents, and critics like Todd think nothing of scanning an anapæst in the place of one of Johnson's feet. Nor can the classical scholar be satisfied ; for even granting that English metrical feet may be classified as tribrachs, dactyls, anapæsts, choriambics, and so forth, there is no classical precedent for versification which indiscriminately admitted all these kinds. The Greek comic metre is the only parallel of anything like closeness ; and, even there, limits were fixed beyond which the poet dare not venture. Such licences as Milton allowed himself in his sublime epic would have been inadmissible in the dialogue of the Frogs, and would have been utterly abhorrent to the laws of the Sophoclean Iambic. The unlearned English reader meanwhile will justly condemn this talk about anapæsts and choriambi as inappropriate. It cannot help him to perceive the melody of a line to be told " here is a trochee," or " there I think I detect an amphibrach ; " for although these terms may usefully be employed between students accustomed to metrical analysis, they do not solve the problem of blank verse. With classical versification the case is different. Quantity determines every line; a long syllable is unmistakable, and invariably weighs as equal in the scale against two short ones. But nothing so definite can be established in English metre. What one man reads as a dactyl may seem like an anapæst or a tribrach to another. So little is our language subject to the laws of quantity, that to have produced four stanzas of decently correct English alcaics is one of the proudest *tours de force* of the most ingenious of our versifiers since Pope. Since therefore quantity forms no part at present of our prosody, and since the licences of quantity in blank verse can never have been determined, it is plainly not much to the purpose to talk about choriambs in Milton. They are undoubtedly to be found there. Our daily speech is larded with trochees and cretics and so forth. But these names of classic feet do not explain the secret of the varied melody of Milton. In order to show the uncertainty which attends the analysis of blank verse on these principles, it is enough to mention that Sir Egerton Brydges scans the line already quoted thus :

' Pārtă | kĕrs, ānd | ūncrōpt | fālls tŏ thĕ | grōund,

"first an iambic ; second, an iambic ; third, a spondee ; fourth, a dactyl ; fifth, a demifoot." He makes no mention of the choriamb, which seemed so evident to Todd, while Keightley, who has written learnedly in the same spirit, seems to reject spondees from his system.

Though the attempt to apply the phraseology of Greek and Latin prosody to the analysis of blank verse is not really satisfactory, yet the principle of substitution of other feet for iambs, asserted by Todd, Brydges, and Keightley, in opposition to Johnson, was a step forward. They defend Milton's irregularities by saying that in the place of two iambs he uses one choriambus, and that he employs trochees, anapæsts, and tribrachs, under certain limitations, as freely as iambs. If these critics had advanced beyond the nomenclature of classic prosody, this principle of substitution would probably have led to a better understanding of the matter. English blank verse really consists of periods of lines, each one of which is made up normally of ten syllables, a stress or accent being thrown upon the final syllable in the line, so that the whole inclines to the iambic rather than to any other rhythm. The ten syllables are, also, if normally cadenced, so disposed that five beats occur in the verse at regular intervals. So far Johnson was right; but he went wrong the instant he proceeded to declare that deviation from this ideal structure of the line produced an inharmonious result. In truth, it is precisely such deviation that constitutes the beauty of blank verse. When the metre was first practised by Surrey, Sackville, Greene, and Peele, great hesitation was displayed as to any departure from iambic regularity ; but Marlowe, the earliest poet of creative genius who applied himself to its cultivation, saw that in order to save the verse from monotony it was necessary to shift the accent, and, playing freely with feet properly so called, to be only careful to preserve the right proportions and masses of sound. A verse may often have more than ten syllables, and more or less than five accents ; but it must carry so much sound as shall be a satisfactory equivalent for ten syllables, and must have its accents so arranged as to content an ear prepared for five. There

are thirteen syllables, and who shall exactly say
how many accents, in this line ?—

> Ruining along the illimitable inane;

yet it quite fulfils the conditions of a good
blank verse. The ponderous

> Showers, hails, snows, frosts, and two-edged winds that
> prime,

which has perhaps seven accents, is as legitimate as the light and rapid—

> Athens, the eye of Greece, mother of arts.

The secret of complex and melodious blank
verse lies in preserving the balance and proportion of syllables, while varying their accent
and their relative weight and volume, so that
each line in a period shall carry its proper
burden of sound, but the burden shall be
differently distributed in the successive verses.
This is done by sometimes allowing two
syllables to take the time of one, and sometimes extending one syllable to the length of
two, by forcing the accentuation of prominent
monosyllables and gliding over successive

liquid sounds, by packing one line with emphatic words so as to retard its movement, by winging another with light and hurried polysyllables, and by so adapting words to sense, and sense to rhythm, that pauses, prolongations, and accelerations, absolutely necessary for the understanding of the matter, evoke a cadence of apparently unstudied melody. In this prosody the bars of the musical composer, where different values from the breve to the demi-semiquaver find their place, suggests perhaps a truer basis of measurement than the longs and shorts of classic quantity. The following line from Milton (" Paradise Regained," iii. 256):

The one winding, the other straight, and left between,

affords a good instance of what is meant by the massing of sounds together, so as to produce a whole harmonious to the ear, but beyond the reach of satisfactory analysis by feet. It is not an Alexandrine, though, if we read it syllabically, it may be made to seem to have six feet. Two groups of syllables—

BLANK VERSE

The one winding | the other straight |

—take up the time of six syllables, and the
verse falls at the end into the legitimate
iambic cadence. At the same time it would
no doubt be possible, by the application of
a Procrustean method of elisions and forcible
divisions, to reduce it to an inexact iambic,
thus :

Th' one win | ding th' oth | er straight. |

This instance suggests the consideration of
another point all-important in the prosody of
blank verse. It is clear that in the line just
quoted the sense helps the sound, and leads the
ear to mass the first eight syllables into the two
groups requisite for the rhythm of the verse.
And this is not only once or occasionally,
but always and invariably the case in all
blank verse composed with proper freedom.
In this respect the metre is true to its original
purpose. It was formed for the drama, where
it had to be the plastic vehicle of every
utterance, and where a perfectly elastic adaptation of the rhythm to the current of the sense

was indispensable. The irregularities in its structure were the natural result of emphasis. This is illustrated by a line of Marlowe, as admirable for its energy of movement as for its imagery :

See where Christ's blood *streams* in the firmament.

That violent stress upon the verb was illegitimate according to iambic scansion; but the verb required emphasis, and the verse gained rather than lost by the deviation from its even rise and fall. The one sound rule to be given to the readers of dramatic blank verse, written by a master of the art, is this : Attend strictly to the sense and to the pauses; the lines will then be perfectly melodious; but if you attempt to scan the lines on any preconceived metrical system, you will violate the sense and vitiate the music. Even the abstruse and fantastic audacities of Webster, who is the veriest Schumann of blank verse, melt into melody when subjected to this simple process. If one does but conceive the dramatic situation, sympathise with the passions of the speaker, allow for the natural inflections of his voice, mark his pauses, and interpolate his inarticulate exclamations, the whole apparently disjointed mass of words assumes a proper and majestic cadence. Milton took blank verse from the dramatists, and practised dramatic blank verse in " Comus "; nor in his epic did he depart from the rules of composition we have analysed. The movement of the sense invariably controlled the rhythm of the verse ; and most of his amorphous lines take form when treated as the products of dramatic art. The following, for example, is one of those that puzzled Johnson, although it is comparatively regular :

'Tis true, I am that Spirit unfortunate.

Johnson, searching for iambs, had not gazed into the fallen Archangel's face—his disguise thrown off, his policy abandoned—nor heard the low slow accents of the two first syllables, the proud emphasis upon the fourth, the stately and melancholy music-roll which closed the line. Yet, in order to understand the rhythm of the verse as the poet wrote it, it was necessary to have heard and seen the fiend as Milton heard and saw. The same may be said about the spasms of intense emotion which have to be imagined in order to give its metrical value to this verse :

Me, me only, just object of his ire.

It is obvious here that scansion by feet will be of little use, though we may grant that the line opens with a spondee followed by a trochee. Its intention is understood as soon as we allow the time of two whole syllables to the first emphatic *me*, and bring over the next words, *me only*, in the time of another two syllables, by doing which we give dramatic energy to the utterance. The truth of this method is still more evident when we take for analysis a verse from the eighth book of " Paradise Lost," at first sight singularly inharmonious :

Submiss; he reared me, and, " Whom thou soughtest, I am."

Try to scan the line, and it seems a confusion of uncertain feet. Read it over by itself, and its packed consonants offend the ear. But now supply the context:

> Rejoicing, but with awe,
> In adoration at his feet I fell
> Submiss; he reared me, and, " Whom thou soughtest,
>   I am,"
> Said mildly, " Author of all this thou seest
> Above, or round about thee, or beneath."—P. L. viii. 319.

It is now seen that the word *submiss* belongs by the sense to the preceding period; the words, *he reared me,* are a parenthesis of quick and hurried narration; then another period commences. So dependent is sound on sense, and so inextricably linked together are the periods in a complex structure of blank verse. It not unfrequently happens that a portion at least of the sound belonging to a word at the commencement of a verse is owed to the cadence of the preceding lines, so that the strain of music which begins is wedded to that which dies, by indescribable and almost imperceptible interpenetrations. The rhythmic dance may therefore be prolonged through sequences and systems of melody, each perfect in itself, each owing and lending something to that which follows and which went before, through concords and affinities of modulated sound.

Notwithstanding the pliancy of the method here suggested for the explanation of Miltonic verse, it is not easy to see the right rhythm of some few of his lines. The following present peculiar difficulties: since at first they seem like Alexandrines; and yet Milton's ear cannot be accused of letting an Alexandrine pass, nor again have they the right Alexandrine pause; while the striking similarity in the endings of these abnormal verses suggests at least some method in their irregularity :

Imbued, bring to their sweetness no satiety.—P. L., viii. 216.
For solitude sometimes is best society.—P. L., ix, 249.
Such solitude before choicest society.—P. R., i. 302.
And linked itself by carnal sensuality.—" Comus," 474.

The last instance, which is at once explained by pronouncing *sensual'ty* as if it had but three syllables, gives perhaps the key to the others. Though the English usage of words in *iety* precludes their elision to the extent required, we must imagine that Milton sometimes gave to such words as *satiety* and *society* the value of three syllables by treating the *ie* almost as if it were a diphthong. The words would then stand at the end of the lines, each forming a full foot, followed by the licensed redundant syllable. It must, however, be mentioned that, in " Paradise Lost" at least, Milton does not often make use of the hendecasyllabic line, and also that in two instances ("Paradise Lost," viii. 383, and ix. 1007), he uses *society* as a quadrisyllable. The ordinary way of explaining such lines is to say that they have two syllables redundant, which is of course a statement of the fact. But here a difficulty which often meets us in English scansion, owing to the different values given at different times to the same word, has to be faced. *Society* will play its part as two good feet in one line,

and in another will have to do service as a
single foot or its equivalent. The pheno-
menon is common enough in dramatic blank
verse, where accelerated and vehement enunciation justifies it.

It may here be remarked that Milton's
familiarity with what he calls the "various-
measured verse" of the ancient poets, and
with the liquid numbers of the Italian hendecasyllable, determined, to some extent, his treatment of our blank verse. The variety of
cadence and elaborate structure of Virgil's
hexameters no doubt incited him to emulation.
He must have felt that the unincumbered
eloquence, which is suited to the drama, where
perspicuity is indispensable, would be out of
place in the stationary and sonorous epic.
Therefore, without seeking to reconstruct in
English the metres of the ancients, he adapted
the complex harmonies of the Roman poets to
the qualities of our language. Like Virgil, he
opened his paragraphs in the middle of a
line, sustaining them through several clauses,

till they reached their close in another hemistich at the distance of some half a dozen carefully conducted verses. His pauses, therefore, are of the greatest importance in regulating his music. From the Italians, again, he learned some secrets in the distribution of equivalent masses of sound. Milton's elisions, and other so-called irregularities, have affinities with the prosody of Dante; for while the normal Italian hendecasyllable runs thus :

Mo su, mo giù, e mo ricirculando,

the poet of the "Inferno" dares to write :

Bestemmiavano Iddio e i lor parenti ;

which is an audacity on a level with many of Milton's.

Two elements of harmony in verse remain to be considered, each of which constitutes a large portion of Milton's music, and without which his pompous rhythm would often be hard and frigid. These are alliteration and assonance. Alliteration is the repetition of the same consonant at the beginning of words in a sentence. Assonance is the repetition of the same vowel in words which do not rhyme strictly. It is well known that the northern nations employed alliteration and not rhyme as the element of melody in poetry. The Vision of Piers Ploughman, for example, is written in a metre of which this is a specimen :

> In habit as a harmot unholy of works
> Went wide in the world wonders to hear.

Assonance, again, is used by the Spanish poets in the place of the fuller rhyme required by our ear. Words like *pain* and *flare* are assonantal. The brief mention of these facts proves that alliteration and assonance can satisfy the craving for repeated sounds in poetry to which modern ears are subject; since each of them has taken the place of rhyme in systematically cultivated literatures. It cannot be denied that the singsong jingle of the alliterative couplet just quoted is intolerable to an educated sense; and it is on this account that alliteration has fallen into general disrepute. Nothing is easier than to turn it to ridicule.

BLANK VERSE

When Shakspere, in "Love's Labour's Lost,"
made Master Holofernes say :

> I will something affect the letter, for it argues facility ;
> The preyful princess pierced and pricked a pretty
> pleasing pricket,

he threw contempt upon the vulgar and
illiterate abusers of an ornament they did not
understand. Nothing, again, is easier than
to make verses that skip or hobble on alliterative crutches. Our ears are wearied with
periods like the following :

> Creeps through a throbbing light that grows and glows
> From glare to greater glare, until it gluts,
> And gulfs him in.

Yet in spite of all this the lofty muse of
Milton owes no small portion of her charm
to this adornment. In order to understand
the Miltonic use of alliteration, it must be
remarked that the faults of the verses just
quoted are due to the alliteration being forced
upon the ear. It is loud and strident, not
flattering the sense by delicate suggestion
and subtle echoes of recurring sound, but

taking it by storm and strumming, as it were, relentlessly upon one nerve. In good alliterative structures the letters chime in at intervals: two or three consonantal sounds are started together, and their recurrences are interwoven like the rhymes in *terza rima*. Here is an instance :

> Far off from these a slow and silent stream,
> Lethe, the river of oblivion, rolls
> Her watery labyrinth, whereof who drinks
> Forthwith his former state and being forgets,
> Forgets both joy and grief, pleasure and pain.
>
> P. L., ii. 582.

Here the letters *f* and *l* predominate ; but they are assisted by alliterations of *s* and *r* and *w* and *g*. Next, it may be shown that really melodious alliteration owes much to medial and final as well as to initial consonants, and also to the admixture of cognate letters, such as *p* or *t* in structures where *b* or *d* predominate. The first of these points is illustrated by a strongly alliterative passage in "Paradise Lost" (v. 322), where, however, it must be admitted that Milton has erred into alliterative monotony:

Small store will serve, where store,
All seasons, ripe for use hangs on the stalk;
Save what by frugal storing firmness gains
To nourish, and superfluous moist consumes.

It will here be noticed that the sibilants, wherever they occur, whether at the beginning, the middle, or the end of the words, are felt. It is rare to find a structure of repeated *s* in Milton.* Some letters lend themselves more than others to harmonious alliteration, and Milton shows decided preference for *f, l, m, r,* and *w. D* and *h* are letters which he uses not always with melodious effect, as in the following passage :

But, lest his heart exalt him in the harm
Already done, to have dispeopled heaven,
My damage fondly deemed, I can repair
That detriment.—P. L., vii. 150.

We may compare, with the two examples just given, those in which mere liquid sounds are employed, even though profusely, so as to observe how far more delicate is the music of the verse. Here is a sequence of *f* and *l*:

* See, however, P. L., vii. 295.

Fairer than feigned of old, or fabled since
Of faery damsels, met in forests wide
By knights of Logres, or of Lyones,
Lancelot or Pelleas or Pellenore.—P. R., ii. 358.

Here is one in which *w* predominates :

Sails between worlds and worlds with steady wing,
Now on the polar winds, then with quick fan
Winnows the buxom air; till within soar
Of towering eagles to all the fowls he seems
A phœnix.—P. L., v. 268.

Three other instances of very marked alliteration may be pointed out, to prove the frequence of repeated sounds which Milton sometimes allowed himself.   They are as follows :

War wearied hath performed what war can do,
And to disordered rage let loose the reins,
With mountains as with weapons armed, which makes
Wild work in heaven and dangerous to the main.

> P. L., vi. 695.

But drive far off the barbarous dissonance
Of Bacchus and his revellers, the race
Of that wild rout that tore the Thracian bard
In Rhodopé, where woods and rocks had ears
To rapture.—P. L., vii. 32.

Moon that now meetest the orient sun, now fliest,
With the fixed stars, fixed in their orb that flies;
And ye five other wandering fires, that move
In mystic dance not without song.—P. L., v. 175.

To these may be added " Paradise Lost," vi. 37–55, a fine instance of interlinked alliterations, *f, r, l, m, p, b,* determining the structure ; while in "Paradise Lost" (vi. 386–405) we find a similar system of *d, f, r, p, v.* The famous passage at the end of the fifth book, which describes the retirement of Abdiel from the rebel army, exhibits splendid alliterative qualities in combination with Milton's favourite sequence of adjectives beginning with *un.*

Another point, besides the interlacement of sounds and intervention of subsidiary letters, which have been already mentioned, characterises the alliteration of Milton. He confines his alliterative systems to periods of sense and metrical construction. When the period is closed, and the thought which it conveys has been expressed, the predominant letter is dropped. Thus there subsists an intimate connection between the metrical melody and the alliterative harmony, both aiding the rhetorical development of the sense. It consequently often happens that the alliteration is descriptive or picturesque, as in the lines about the Parthian bowmen :

> Flying behind them shot
> Sharp sleet of arrowy showers against the face
> Of their pursuers.
>
> P. R., iii. 323 (cf. P. L., vi. 211–213).

The descriptive pomp of the alliterative system is more remarkable in the passage where Raphael relates the division of earth from water :

> Immediately the mountains huge appear,
> Emergent, and their broad bare backs upheave
> Into the clouds ; their tops ascend the sky,
> So high as heaved the tumid hills, so low
> Down sunk a hollow bottom, broad and deep,
> Capacious bed of waters. Thither they
> Hasted with glad precipitance, up-rolled,
> As drops on dust conglobing, from the dry ;
> Part rise in crystal wall, or ridge direct,
> For haste ; such flight the great command im-
>   pressed
> On the swift floods. As armies at the call
> Of trumpet—for of armies thou hast heard—
> Troop to their standard, so the watery throng,
> Wave rolling after wave, where way they found ;
> If steep, with torrent rapture, if through plain,
> Soft-ebbing : nor withstood them rock or hill ;
> But they, or underground, or circuit wide

With serpent error wandering, found their way,
And on the washy ooze deep channels wore.

P. L., vii. 285–303.

Here the letters *b* and *h*, not inaptly, mark the firmness and resistance of the earth, while *w* and *r* depict the liquid lapse of waters.

Enough, perhaps, has now been said to prove that the harmony of Milton's verse depends very greatly upon alliteration ; and here it may be observed that he not unfrequently repeats the same word, as much with a view to the recurrence of sound, as with a rhetorical intention. In " Paradise Regained" (iii. 109) there is a period of twelve lines in which we find the word *glory* eight times repeated, and the alliteration strengthened by five subsidiary *g's*. At the 205th line of the same book, there is a period of six verses containing *worse* five times, supported by three subsidiary *w's*. In each of these cases the repetition is of course rhetorically studied. A very remarkable instance of the grandeur resulting from simple reiteration is the following :

BLANK VERSE

If I foreknew,
Foreknowledge had no influence on their fault;
Which had no less proved certain unforeknown.

P. L., iii. 117.

The assonance of various forms of the *o* sound adds to the volume of the music in these lines.

Assonance, though not so obvious as alliteration, is no less potent. Of its place in Milton's versification something must be said.* To begin with, the poet was himself very sensitive to the harmony of vowel sounds when well pronounced. In his Epistle to Master Hartlib, he lays it down as a rule that, in the education of youths, "their speech is to be fashioned to a distinct and clear pronunciation, as near as may be to the Italian, especially in the vowels. For we Englishmen, being far northerly, do not open our mouths in the cold air wide enough to grace a southern tongue," &c. His blank verse

---

* This also would be the place to discuss the occasional rhymes found in Milton's blank verse. P. L., xi. 853–860, has no less than six assonantal endings. See, too, P. L., iv. 957; P. L., i. 612.

abounds in open-mouthed, deep-chested *a's*
and *o's.* Here is a passage in which their
assonance is all the more remarkable from the
absence of alliteration :

> Say, Goddess, what ensued when Raphael,
> The affable Archangel, had forewarned
> Adam, by dire example, to beware
> Apostasy, by what befell in Heaven
> To those apostates; lest the like befall
> In Paradise to Adam or his race,
> Charged not to touch the interdicted tree, &c.
>
> P. L., vii. 40.

The opening lines of Book ii., the passage
about Mulciber at the end of Book i., and
the great symphonious period which describes
the movement of the fallen angels " to the
Dorian mood of flutes and soft recorders,"
all serve to illustrate the gorgeousness of
Milton's assonance. In attempting to charac-
terise the effect of these deep-toned vowels,
it is almost necessary to borrow words from
the art of colours, since what colours are to
painting vowels are to verse. It would seem,
after drinking in draught after draught of
these intoxicating melodies, as if Milton with

unerring tact had selected from the English
language only such words as are pompous,
full-sounding, capable of being wrought into
the liquid architecture of articulate music.
Discord, who is so busy in the lines of even
mighty poets, stands apart and keeps silence
here. That tenuity of sound and want of
volume from which the periods of otherwise
great versifiers occasionally suffer, never occurs
in Milton. Like Virgil he is unerringly and
unremittingly harmonious. Music is the
element in which his genius lives, just as
light is the element of Pindar, or as darkness
covers the "Inferno" like a pall.

Having attempted an analysis of the melody
of Milton's blank verse, it remains to speak
about the changes which may be traced in
it from the date of " Comus " to that of
"Samson Agonistes." "Comus," as might
have been expected both from the time of
its composition and its form, is the one of
Milton's masterpieces in which he has adhered
most closely to the traditions of the Eliza-

bethan drama. His style, it is true, is already
more complex and peculiarly harmonious, more
characteristically Miltonic, than that of any of
the dramatists. Yet there are passages in
"Comus" which remind us forcibly of
Fletcher. Others, like the following :

> How sweetly did they float upon the wings
> Of silence, through the empty vaulted night!
> At every fall smoothing the raven down
> Of darkness till it smiled,

might have been written by Shakspere. Alliteration is used freely, but more after the
manner of Fletcher or of Spenser, not with the
sustained elaboration of Milton's maturity.
The truly Miltonic licences are rare ; we find
fewer inverted sentences, less lengthy systems
of concatenated periods—in a word, a more
fluent and simpler versification. Both in the
imagery and the melody of "Comus" there
is youthful freshness, an almost wanton dis-
play of vernal bloom and beauty. In the
"Paradise Lost" we reach the manhood of the
art of Milton. His elaborate metrical structure,
supported by rich alliteration and assonance,

here attains its full development. Already too there is more of rugged and abrupt sublimity in the blank verse of the " Paradise Lost " than can be found in that of " Comus." The metre, learned in the school of the Elizabethan drama, is being used in accordance with the models of the Roman Epic. Yet the fancy of the poet has not yet grown chill or lost luxuriance, nor has his ear become less sensitive to every musical modulation of which our language is capable. " Paradise Regained " presents a marked change. Except in descriptive passages, there is but little alliterative melody ; while all the harsh inversions and rugged eccentricities of abnormally constructed verses are retained. It is noticeable that hendecasyllabic lines, which are but sparingly used in " Paradise Lost," only two occurring in the first book, become frequent in " Paradise Regained," and add considerably to the heaviness of its movement. These, for example, are found within a short space in the first book :

BLANK VERSE

One day forth walked alone, the Spirit leading. . . . .
Awakened in me swarm, while I consider. . . . .
These gnawing thoughts my mother soon perceiving. . . . .
A star not seen before in heaven appearing. . . . .

No doubt there are admirers of Milton who would not allow that the metrical changes in " Paradise Regained " are for the worse. Yet it is hardly to be denied that, in comparison with the " Paradise Lost," much of richness, variety, sonorousness, and liquid melody has been sacrificed. " Samson Agonistes " is a step beyond " Paradise Regained " in dryness, ruggedness, and uncompromising severity. The blank verse is shorn of alliterative and assonantal harmony, except in the last speech of Manoah, and in a few of the more pensive passages scattered up and down the drama. Still it displays every form of the true Miltonic metre in so far as audacities of accent and accumulations of compacted syllables are concerned. To the lover of the most exalted poetry, " Samson Agonistes," even as regards its versification, may possibly offer a pleasure more subtle, and more rare than " Paradise

Lost," with all its full-toned harmonies. It has the grandeur of a play of Sophocles which after passing through the medium of the Latin genius, has been committed to English by the loftiest of modern poets in austere old age. "Comus" shows the style of the master in his earliest manhood, with the luxuriance of an untamed youth, the labyrinthine blossoms of an unpruned fancy. "Paradise Lost" exhibits the same richness, mellowed by age and subordinated to the laws of abstruse and deeply studied proportion. In "Paradise Regained" the master has grown older, and his taste is more severe. In "Samson Agonistes" colour and melody have lost their charm for him, though he preserves his mighty style, restraining it within limits prescribed by a taste ascetically grave. In "Comus" we have the glowing hues of a Giorgione, with a comparatively weak design. In "Paradise Lost" the design of a Michelangelo is added to the colouring of a Titian. In "Paradise Regained" both colour and design are of the great Florentine. In "Samson Agonistes" the design is still that of Michelangelo ; but the picture is executed *en grisaille*, in severest chiaroscuro, careful only of the form. Fortunately we know the dates of Milton's masterpieces. There is therefore no uncertainty or subjectivity of criticism in the analysis of these changes in his manner ; at the same time they are precisely what we might have expected *a priori*—the intellectual gaining on the sensual qualities of art as the poet advanced in age.